1·2·3 Draw
CARTOON MONSTERS

A step-by-step guide

by Steve Barr

Peel Productions, Inc

This book is dedicated to my cousins, Judy and Kenn Dean, to thank them for always making me laugh and smile. Judy and I spent one of the best summers of our lives working as monsters in a haunted house on the boardwalk!

-S.B.

Published by Peel Productions, Inc.
Printed in China

Library of Congress Cataloging-in-Publication Data
Barr, Steve, 1958-
  1-2-3 draw cartoon monsters : a step-by-step guide / by Steve Barr.
    p. cm. -- (1-2-3 draw)
   ISBN 0-939217-74-0 (alk. paper)
1. Cartooning--Technique--Juvenile literature. 2. Monsters in
art--Juvenile literature. [1. Cartooning--Technique. 2. Monsters in
art.] I. Title: Cartoon monsters. II. Title.
NC1764.8.M65 B37 2004
741.5--dc22

Distributed to the trade and art markets in North America by

NORTH LIGHT BOOKS,
an imprint of F&W Publications, Inc.
4700 East Galbraith Road
Cincinnati, OH 45236

(800) 289-0963

Table of Contents

Before you begin
Stop! Look! Listen!

You will need:

1. a sharpened pencil
2. paper
3. an eraser
4. a pencil sharpener
5. colored pencils, markers or crayons
6. a comfortable place to sit and draw
7. a good light source

Now, let's begin!

NO rules!

This book is designed to teach you the basics of cartoon drawing. There are no rules about cartoon monsters! Doodle, experiment, and change the drawings in this book to make them your very own! Color them any color you choose to.

Sketch, doodle, play!

You can use any shapes you want to make a cartoon. If the instructions tell you to use an oval to draw something and you want to use a square, draw a square. Try out different shapes to see what you can create. Monsters can be big, furry, and friendly, or they can be short, scaly, and grumpy. Explore and experiment as you go through this book. If your drawing makes you smile, you are doing it right!

Cartooning tips:

1 Draw lightly at first—SKETCH, so you can erase extra lines.
2 Practice, practice, practice! You will get better and your cartoons will get funnier.
3 Have FUN cartooning!

Basic Shapes and Lines

Here are the basic shapes and lines
you will use to draw cartoons monsters:

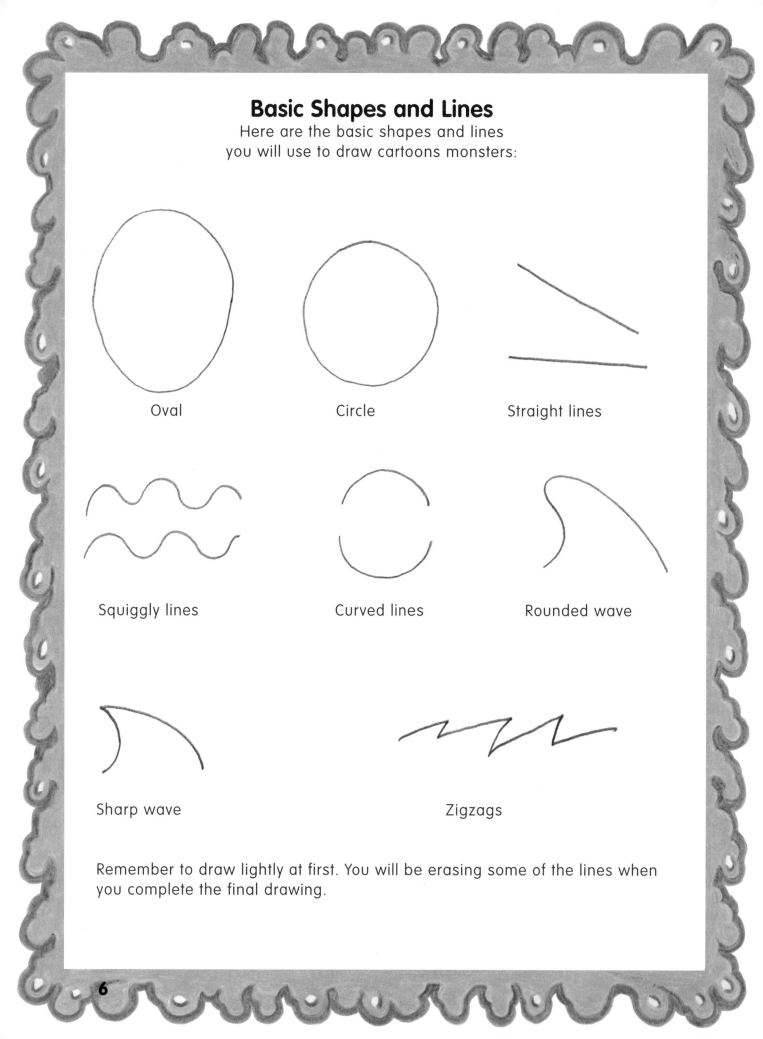

Oval

Circle

Straight lines

Squiggly lines

Curved lines

Rounded wave

Sharp wave

Zigzags

Remember to draw lightly at first. You will be erasing some of the lines when you complete the final drawing.

Monster face (front view)

Let's start with an easy monster face.

1 Lightly sketch an oval. Add a sharp wave shape to each side for the ears.

2 Sketch two ovals for the eyes. Draw curved lines to begin the mouth.

3 Draw curved lines inside the eyes for eyeballs. Add a small curved line to the edge of the mouth.

4 Add curved lines inside each ear. Draw curved lines inside the mouth for teeth.

5 LOOK carefully at the final drawing! Erase extra sketch lines. Darken the final lines. Color your monster.

Great job!

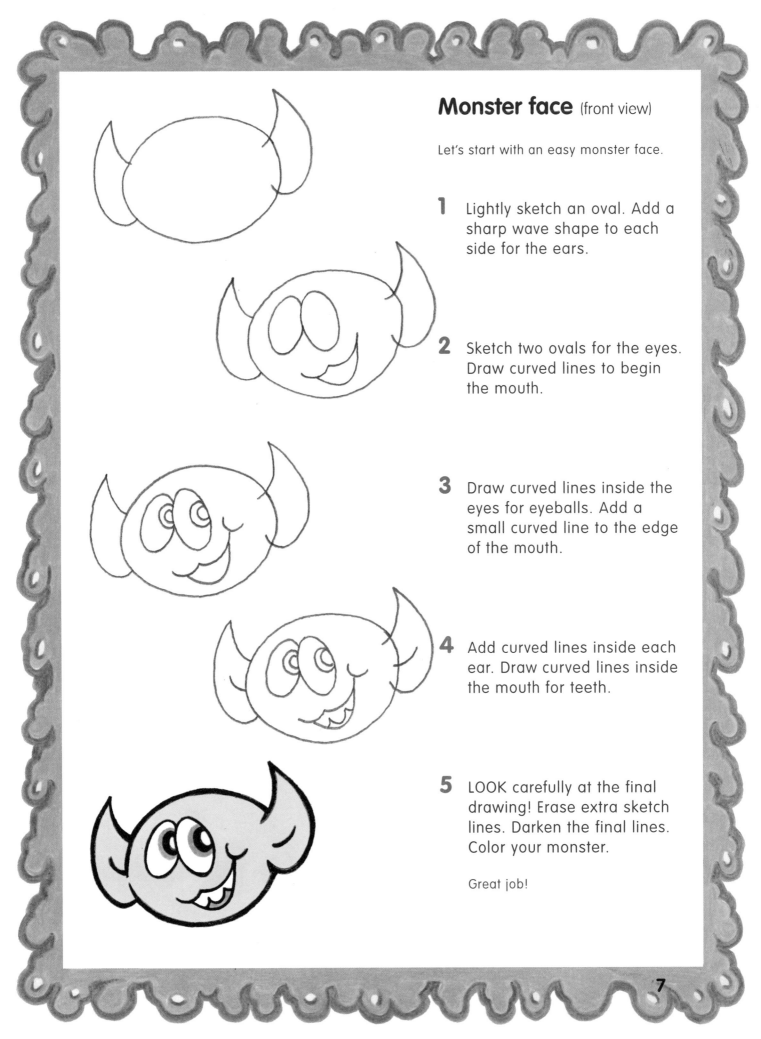

7

Monster face (side view)

Let's draw the side view of a monster face with LOTS of sharp teeth!

1 Sketch a large oval for the head. Add an overlapping oval for the nose. Draw an oval for the eye.

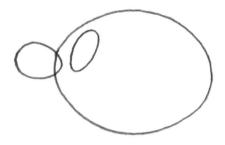

2 Draw two curved lines inside the eye for an eyeball. Add a large sharp wave shape on one side for the ear.

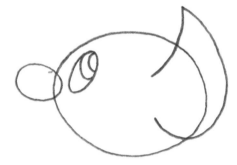

3 Draw two curved lines for a mouth.

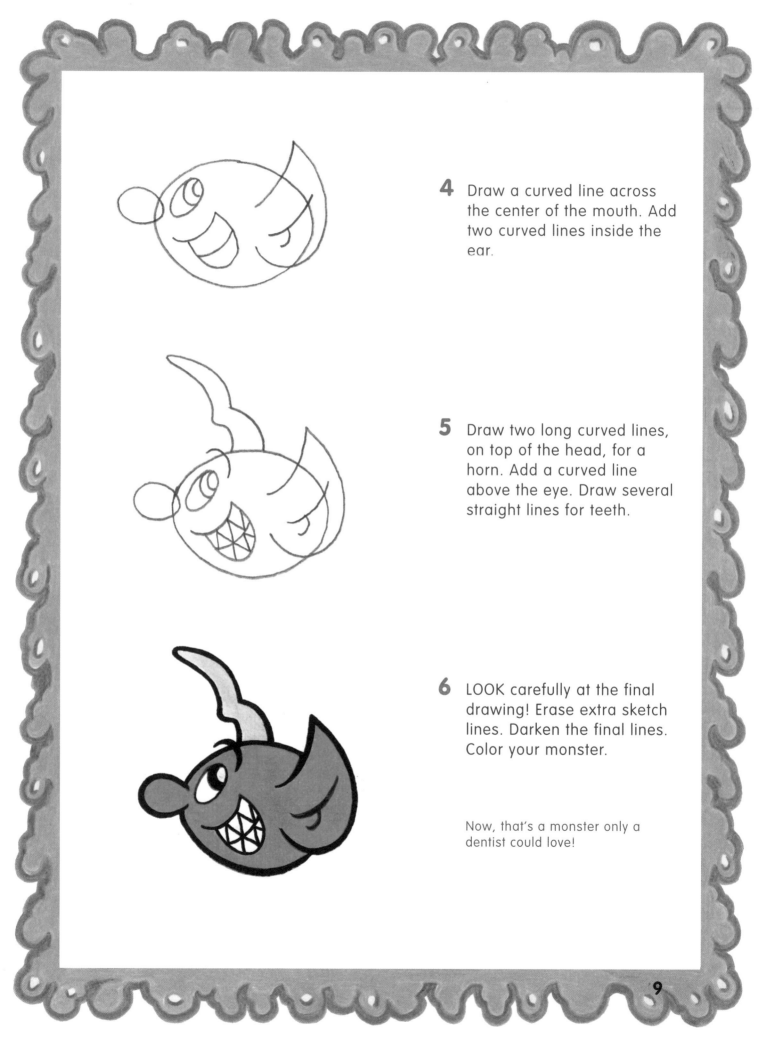

4 Draw a curved line across the center of the mouth. Add two curved lines inside the ear.

5 Draw two long curved lines, on top of the head, for a horn. Add a curved line above the eye. Draw several straight lines for teeth.

6 LOOK carefully at the final drawing! Erase extra sketch lines. Darken the final lines. Color your monster.

Now, that's a monster only a dentist could love!

Grouchy monster face

Let's draw another front view of a grouchy monster face.

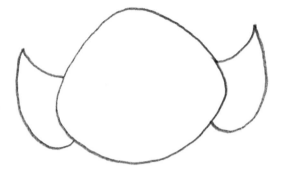

1   Sketch an oval for the head. Draw a sharp wave shape on each side of the oval for ears.

2   Sketch a small oval for a nose. Add a curved line and a straight line for the mouth.

3   Draw sharp wave shapes on top for hair. Add curved lines to each ear. Put a small sharp wave shape on the mouth.

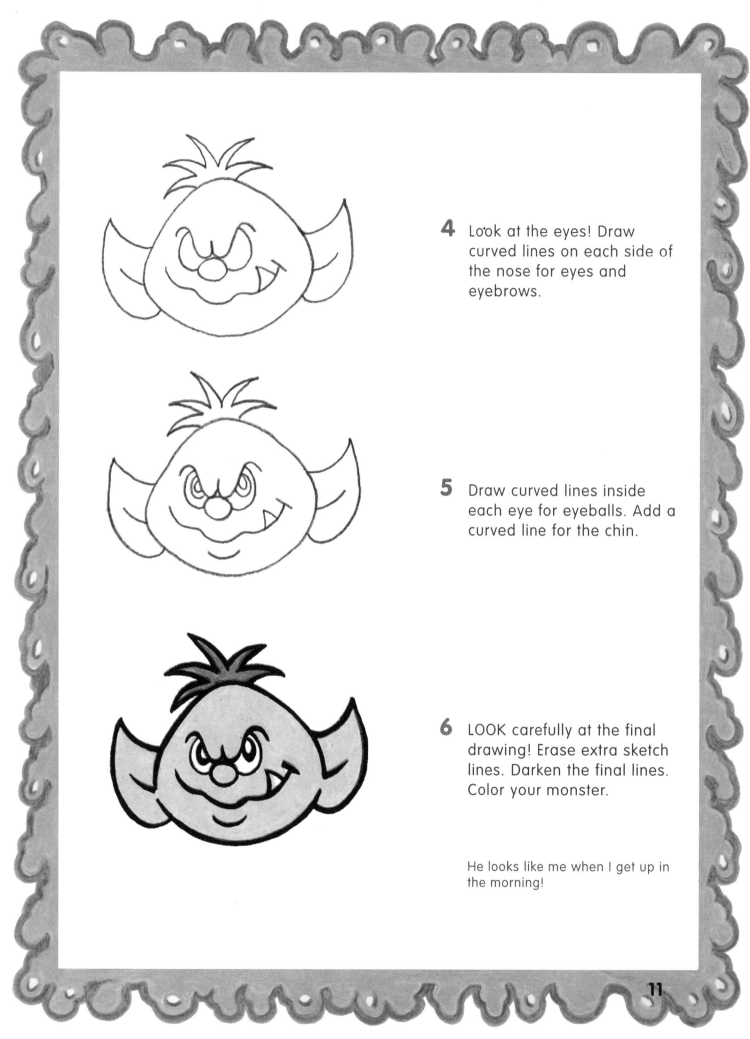

4 Look at the eyes! Draw curved lines on each side of the nose for eyes and eyebrows.

5 Draw curved lines inside each eye for eyeballs. Add a curved line for the chin.

6 LOOK carefully at the final drawing! Erase extra sketch lines. Darken the final lines. Color your monster.

He looks like me when I get up in the morning!

One-eyed monster

Monsters can have one eye or they can have as many as you want to draw. Let's try sketching a one-eyed monster.

1 Sketch two overlapping ovals.

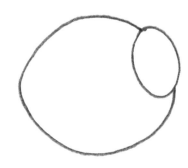

2 Put a small curved line beside the eye. Draw straight lines for legs and curved lines for feet.

3 Sketch a sharp wave shape on the back of the head. Draw an oval and a curved line for an eyeball.

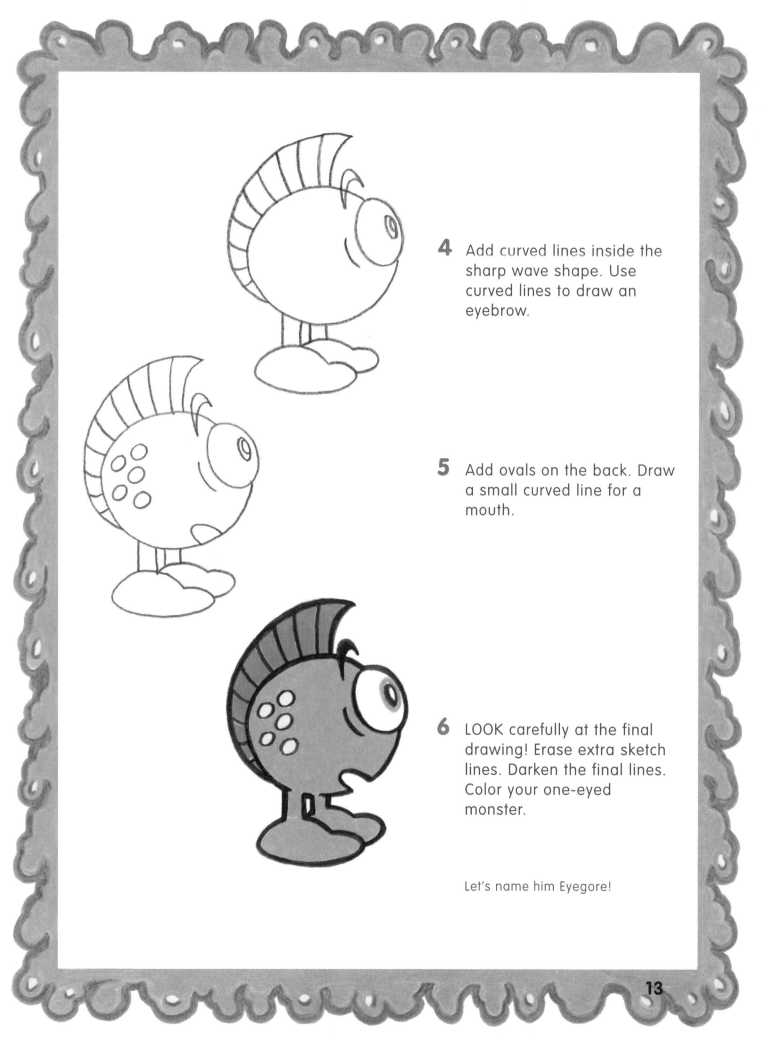

4 Add curved lines inside the sharp wave shape. Use curved lines to draw an eyebrow.

5 Add ovals on the back. Draw a small curved line for a mouth.

6 LOOK carefully at the final drawing! Erase extra sketch lines. Darken the final lines. Color your one-eyed monster.

Let's name him Eyegore!

One-eyed monster's cousin

Not all one-eyed monsters look alike. Let's draw a one-eyed monster that looks different from the one that you just drew.

1 Sketch a squashed oval for the eye. Sketch a larger oval for the body. Draw two curved lines for the neck.

2 Add a curved line inside the eye oval. Draw curved lines for legs. Add overlapping ovals for feet.

3 Draw an oval and a curved line for the eyeball. Draw a curved line across the eye.

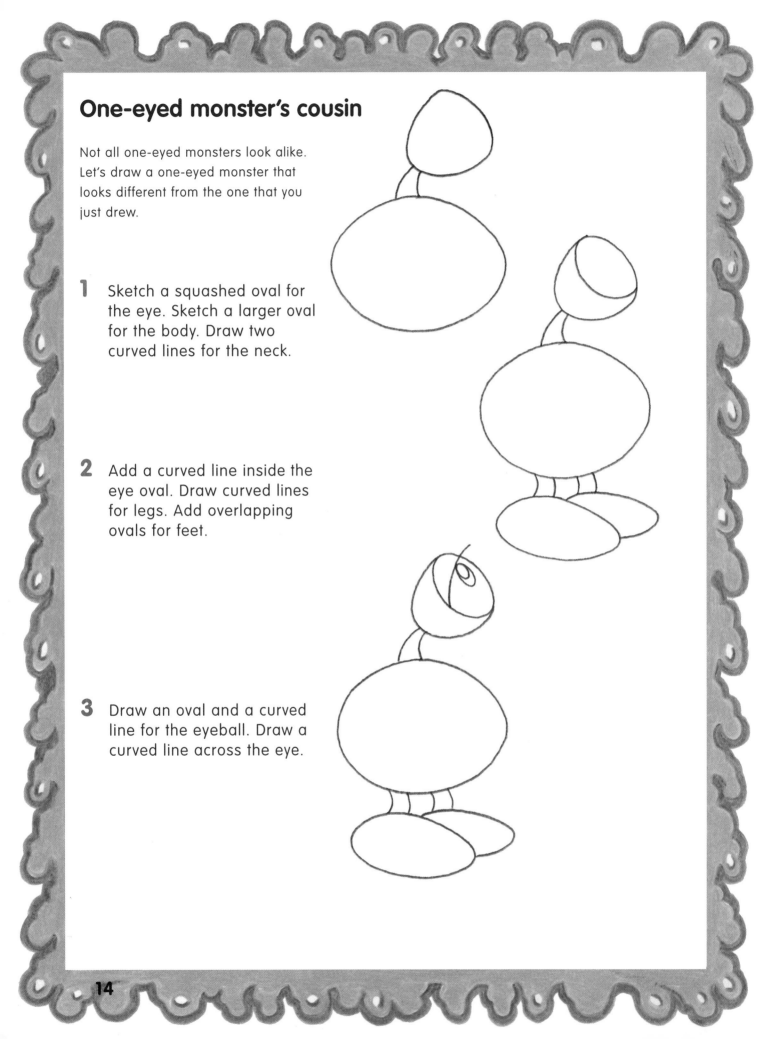

4 Draw curved lines for the smiling mouth.

5 Add ovals and curved lines for spots on the body. Add curved lines inside the mouth.

6 LOOK carefully at the final drawing! Erase extra sketch lines. Darken the final lines. Color your monster.

She's a winner!

Claw monster

Here's a scary little monster with lots of sharp claws. This time you will draw the body, too.

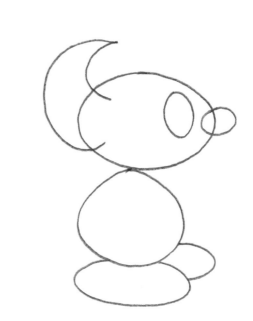

1 Sketch two overlapping ovals for the head and nose. Sketch an oval for the body.

2 Draw a sharp wave shape for an ear. Add an oval for an eye. Draw an oval and a curved line for the feet.

3 Draw two curved lines inside the ear. Add a curved line for an eyebrow. Draw a sharp wave shape for a tail.

4 Add two curved lines for the eyeball. Draw four curved lines to shape the mouth. Draw an oval and a curved line for the arms. Add curved lines for fingers on each arm.

5 Draw sharp wave shapes on top of his head for hair. Add straight lines to his mouth for teeth. Draw sharp wave shapes for finger and toe nails.

6 LOOK carefully at the final drawing! Erase extra sketch lines. Darken the final lines. Color your monster.

If you draw a Santa hat on him, he could be called Santa Claws!

Frankenstein's Monster

First, let's draw the head of Frankenstein's monster.

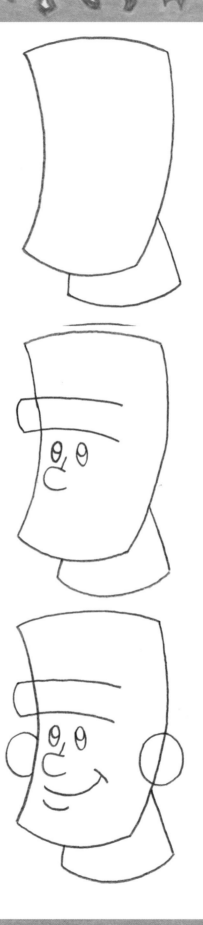

1 Sketch four long curved connecting lines for the head. Add three curved lines below it for the neck.

2 Draw three curved lines for his brow. Draw two ovals for the eyes. Add a curved line inside each. Draw a straight line and a curved line for his nose.

3 Draw a curved line and an oval for the ears. Add curved lines for his mouth.

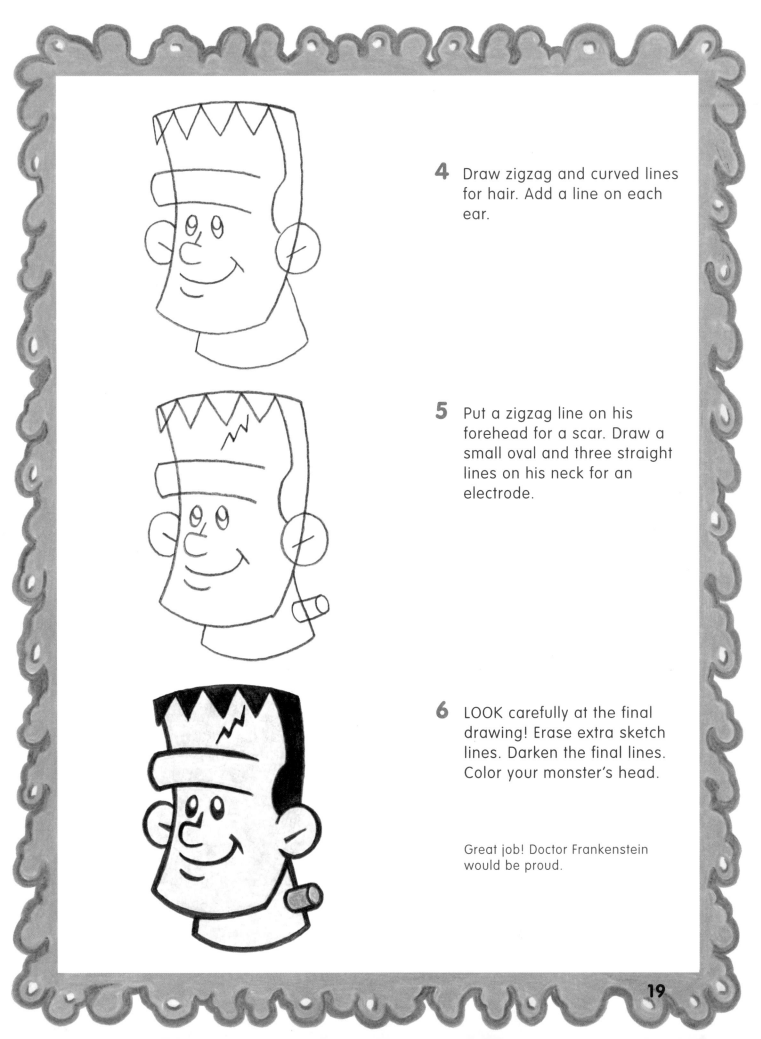

4 Draw zigzag and curved lines for hair. Add a line on each ear.

5 Put a zigzag line on his forehead for a scar. Draw a small oval and three straight lines on his neck for an electrode.

6 LOOK carefully at the final drawing! Erase extra sketch lines. Darken the final lines. Color your monster's head.

Great job! Doctor Frankenstein would be proud.

Let's bring the monster to life by adding a moving body. Start by drawing the head again. Make sure you leave plenty of room at the bottom of your paper to add his body.

1 Draw the monster's head. Look at the body shape. Sketch the outline of his upper body using long curved lines. Draw straight lines for legs.

2 Draw the arms using curved and straight lines. Add ovals for hands. Add curved lines for thumbs. Draw ovals and curved lines for shoes.

3 Add curved lines for fingers. Add two curved lines on each shoe.

4 LOOK carefully at the final drawing! Erase extra sketch lines. Darken the final lines. Color your monster.

Wow! Great monster!

Mummy

Let's draw a friend for Frankenstein's monster.

1   Sketch an oval for the head. Draw curved lines for the body.

2   Sketch curved lines for arms and legs. Add an oval to the bottom of each leg for feet.

3   Draw an oval at the end of each arm for hands. Add curved lines for fingers.

4 Draw a curved line across the center of the head. Add curved lines for eyes and eyeballs.

5 Sketch curved lines all over the body and head for bandages.

6 LOOK carefully at the final drawing! Erase extra sketch lines. Darken the final lines. Color your mummy.

Good job! You wrapped her up nicely!

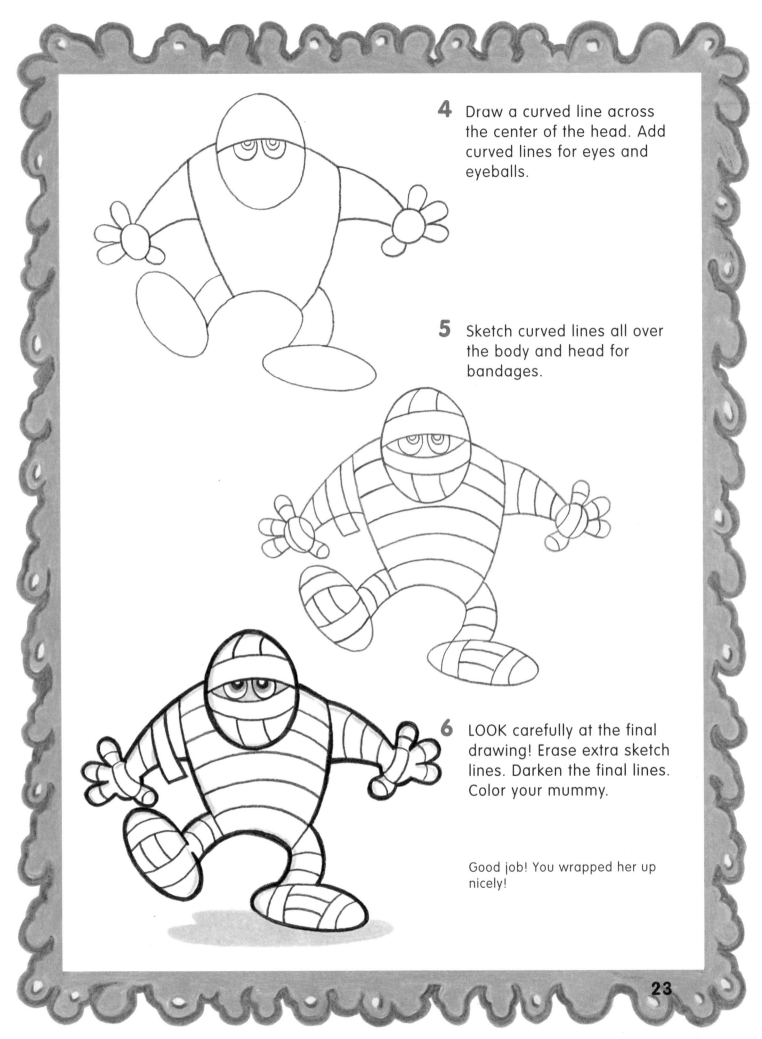

Vampire

One of the scariest monsters is a vampire! Let's draw a cartoon vampire, starting with the head. We'll add the body later.

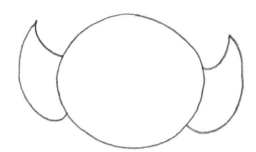

1 Sketch an oval for the head. Add sharp wave shapes to each side.

2 Draw curved lines on top for hair. Add curved lines for eyebrows. Add an oval for the nose.

3 Draw a small oval and a curved line for each eye.

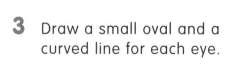

4 Add a curved line inside each ear. Look at the happy mouth. Draw it.

5 Sketch curved lines inside his mouth for teeth and fangs.

6 LOOK carefully at the final drawing! Erase extra sketch lines. Darken the final lines. Color your monster.

He should see a doctor about his coffin!

Count Dracula

Let's give the vampire a body. Start by drawing the head. Leave plenty of room under it to add the body.

1 Draw the vampire's head again. Sketch a large oval for the body. Draw straight lines for legs. Add curved lines for feet.

2 Draw straight lines for arms. Add ovals and curved lines for hands and fingers..

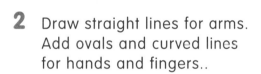

3 Draw long curved lines to make the cape. Add a small circle in the center of the body for a button.

4 Draw a V shape neck line. Add a curved line below the button.

5 Draw lines for a shirt collar and tie.

6 LOOK carefully at the final drawing! Erase extra sketch lines. Darken the final lines. Color your vampire.

Question: What does a vampire never order for dinner?

Answer: A stake!

Hairy Monster

Let's draw a really hairy monster.

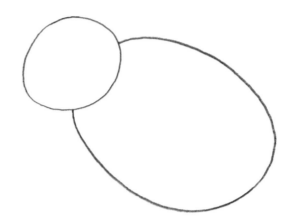

1 Sketch two overlapping ovals.

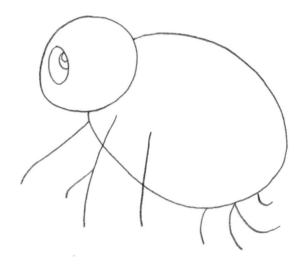

2 Draw an oval and two curved lines for eyes. Sketch curved lines for the four legs.

3 Draw a short curved line for a nose. Add four ovals to the legs for feet.

4 Sketch a squiggly line for a mouth. Add curved lines to the hands for fingers.

5 Add large sharp waves around his head and body for hair. Draw a sharp wave shape for a tooth.

6 LOOK carefully at the final drawing! Erase extra sketch lines. Darken the final lines. Color your big, furry monster.

That's a pretty hairy-looking monster!

Abominable Snowman

Let's draw an awesome Abominable Snowman, otherwise known as a yeti.

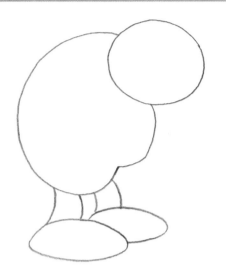

1 Sketch an oval for his head. Draw a long curved line for his body. Add curved lines for legs and feet.

2 Draw an oval and two curved lines for his eye. Sketch two curved lines for his mouth. Add two long curved lines for arms.

3 Sketch an oval for his hand. Draw a curved line for his back arm. Add curved lines for fingers.

4 Draw two curved lines to make his lip and nose. Add a row of curved lines to the top and bottom of his mouth.

5 Sketch small sharp wave shapes around his body. Add a sharp wave shape to each finger for nails.

6 LOOK carefully at the final drawing! Erase extra sketch lines. Darken the final lines. Color your yeti.

Draw some snow around him to make him really look cool!

Swamp Monster

Let's draw a monster made of swamp mush.

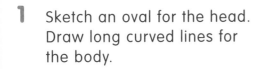

1 Sketch an oval for the head. Draw long curved lines for the body.

2 Draw curved lines to make the nose, eye, and eyebrow. Add curved lines for legs.

3 Starting at the top, add curved lines for the eyeball. Draw straight lines for arms. Add an oval to the end of each leg.

4 Draw curved lines inside his mouth for teeth. Add an oval for hands, and curved lines for fingers.

5 Add curved lines to his head and body for swamp mush. Draw a few raindrop shapes to show the mush falling from his body.

6 LOOK carefully at the final drawing! Erase extra sketch lines. Darken the final lines. Color your monster.

Look out your window to make sure he's not outside mucking about!

Werewolf

A creature of the night, the werewolf can be a scary guy to bump into in the woods. Let's draw one.

1 Sketch an oval for the head. Use long curved lines to make the body. Add curved lines for arms and legs.

2 Draw an oval on the end of each arm and leg. Add curved lines for fingers

3 Draw two ovals for eyes. Add curved lines for eyeballs. Draw an oval for the nose. Add two curved lines for the mouth.

4 Add curved lines for eyebrows. Draw sharp wave shapes for ears. Look at the lines on the feet. Add these.

5 Draw sharp wave shapes around the head and body for hair.

6 LOOK carefully at the final drawing! Erase extra sketch lines. Darken the final lines. Color your werewolf.

Werewolf? There wolf! Great job.

Two-Horned Monster

Usually found hiding under beds, the
two-horned monster is quite a sight!
Let's draw one.

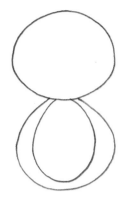

1 Sketch an oval for the head
and two overlapping ovals
for the body.

2 Add long curved lines for
arms, legs and feet.

3 Draw two ovals, with a
curved line in each, for eyes.
Add a circle for the nose.
Draw the happy mouth with
curved lines. Draw straight
lines across the chest.

4 Add small curved lines for teeth. Draw curved lines for fingers and fingernails. Add a curved line to each leg for knees. Use curved lines to add toenails.

5 Use curved lines to draw the horns. Add zigzag lines for hair. Add a curved line inside each ear.

6 LOOK carefully at the final drawing! Erase extra sketch lines. Darken the final lines. Color your monster.

I think I'll sleep on the couch tonight.

Grouchy Monster

Let's draw a grouchy monster from head to toe

1 Sketch an oval for the head and another for the body. Draw two straight lines for the neck. Draw four straight lines for the legs. Add an oval and a curved line for feet.

2 Draw a curved line for a nose. Look at the eye and eyebrow. Use curved lines to draw these. Look at the mouth. Draw two curved lines to form the mouth.

3 Draw sharp wave shapes around his head. Add curved lines for arms. Add an oval for the right hand. Use straight lines to draw the crooked tail.

4 Draw lines across the chest. Using straight lines, make an arrow on the end of the tail.

5 Starting at the top, add sharp teeth. Draw fingers with curved lines. Add lines for fingernails and toenails. Add jagged lines on his tail.

6 LOOK carefully at the final drawing! Erase extra sketch lines. Darken the final lines. Color your monster.

Now that's a grouchy monster!

Ogre

Ogres will leave you alone as long as you don't bother them. I don't think it will bother this ogre if we just sketch his face. We'll draw his body next, if he's agreeable.

1   Sketch an egg-shaped oval for the head. Add sharp wave shapes to each side for ears.

2   Draw two ovals for eyes. Add another oval for the nose.

3   Draw two curved lines above the eyes for eyebrows. Using curved lines, add eyeballs.

4 Add small curved lines inside each ear. Draw curved lines to make the mouth. Add a curved line beside and below the mouth.

5 Add a curved line below one eye. Draw curved lines for the tongue. Draw teeth with straight lines.

6 LOOK carefully at the final drawing! Erase extra sketch lines. Darken the final lines. Color your ogre's face.

That was fun! I could draw him ogre, and ogre, and ogre.

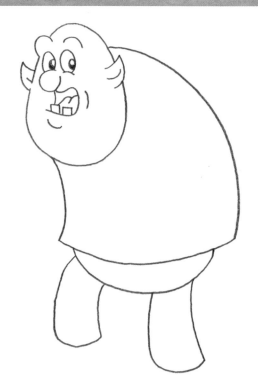

Let's draw an ogre head to toe. Leave room beneath the head to draw the body.

1 Sketch the Ogre face again. Use long curved lines for his upper torso. Add a curved line below his torso. Draw curved lines for legs.

2 Sketch long curved lines for arms. Add ovals to the arms for hands. Draw ovals at the bottoms of his legs.

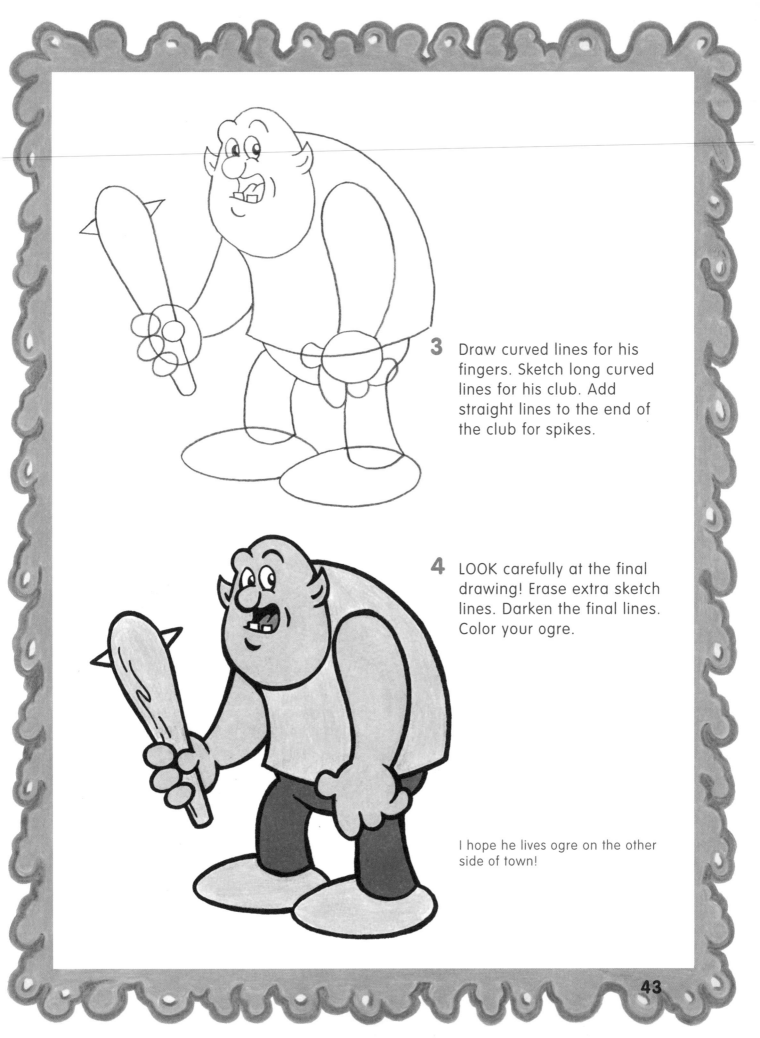

3 Draw curved lines for his fingers. Sketch long curved lines for his club. Add straight lines to the end of the club for spikes.

4 LOOK carefully at the final drawing! Erase extra sketch lines. Darken the final lines. Color your ogre.

I hope he lives ogre on the other side of town!

Monsters Have Feelings Too!

Even monsters have feelings. Here are some simple shapes and lines you can use to add expressions to your drawings. Draw the ogre's face again and try sketching some of these diffirent emotions you see.

Shocked

Happy

Angry

Sad

Tired

Silly

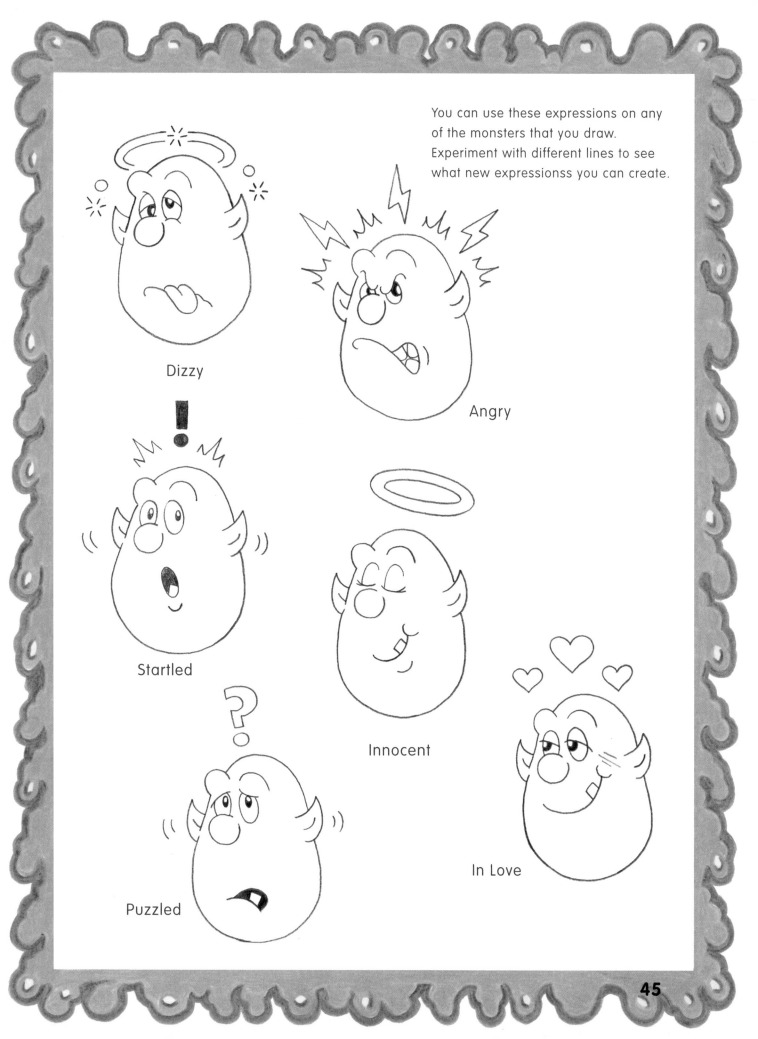

You can use these expressions on any of the monsters that you draw. Experiment with different lines to see what new expressionss you can create.

Dizzy

Angry

Startled

Innocent

Puzzled

In Love

45

Gargoyle

Gargoyles are really cool monsters that turn to stone during the day. They come to life at night and swoop down out of the air. Let's start with a gargoyle face.

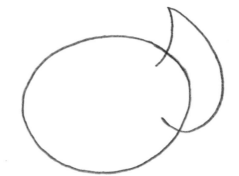

1 Sketch an oval for the head. Draw a sharp wave shape on one side for an ear.

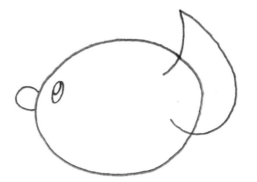

2 Add a curved line for a nose. Draw an oval with a small circle in it, for the eye.

3 Add a curved line above the eye. Draw a sharp wave shape below the nose for a jaw.

4 Look at the mouth. Using curved lines, draw the mouth. Add a small curved line inside the ear.

5 Draw a few small ovals on top of the head for lumps. Add sharp curved lines for teeth.

6 LOOK carefully at the final drawing! Erase extra sketch lines. Darken the final lines. Color your gargoyle's face.

Why did the monster's breath smell funny?

He didn't gargoyle after he brushed his teeth!

He seems happy enough. Now we can make a body for that beautiful gargoyle face! Start by drawing another face, leaving room below it to add the body.

1 Look at the body shape. Using a curved line, draw the body. Add curved lines for legs. Draw an oval and a curved line for the feet.

2 Starting at the top, use sharp wave shapes to make the wings. Add arms and hands with curved lines and ovals.

3 Draw curved lines on the hands for fingers and thumbs. Use two curved lines to make the tail.

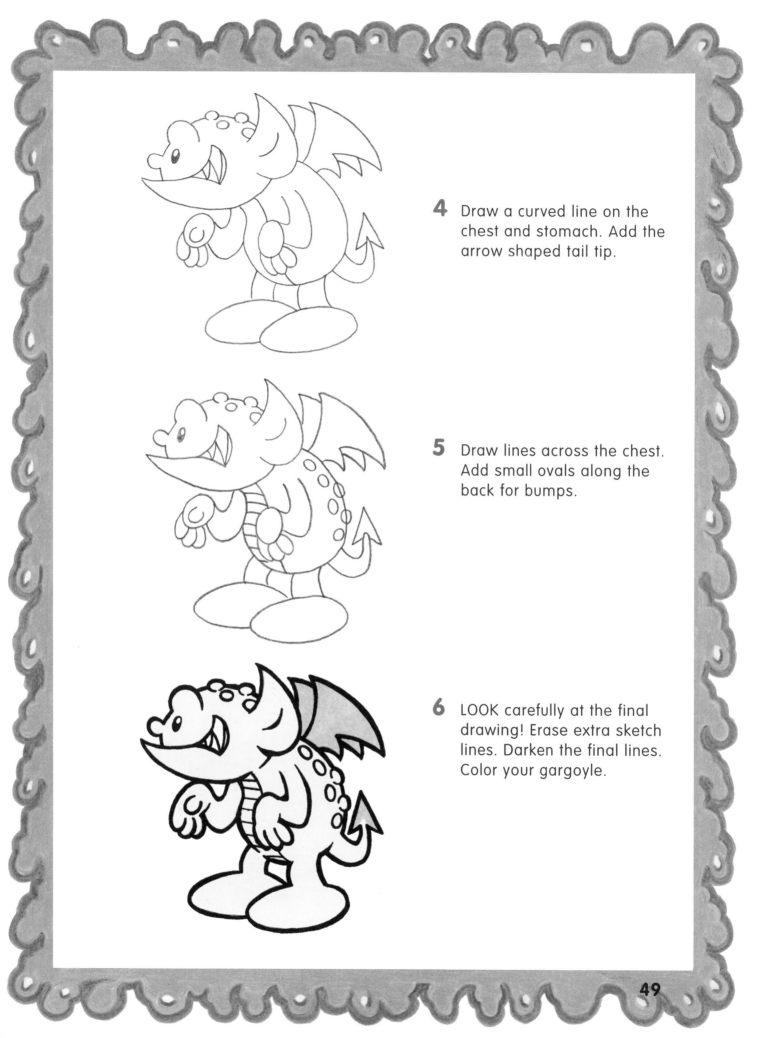

4 Draw a curved line on the chest and stomach. Add the arrow shaped tail tip.

5 Draw lines across the chest. Add small ovals along the back for bumps.

6 LOOK carefully at the final drawing! Erase extra sketch lines. Darken the final lines. Color your gargoyle.

Lizard Monsters

Some monsters look like giant lizards. Let's draw the face of one.

1 Sketch a large oval for the head. Draw two ovals inside for the eyes.

2 Look at the crooked mouth. Add curved lines for the mouth.

3 Draw a curved line above each eye. Draw an oval and a curved line for each eyeball. Add a curved line at the bottom of each eye.

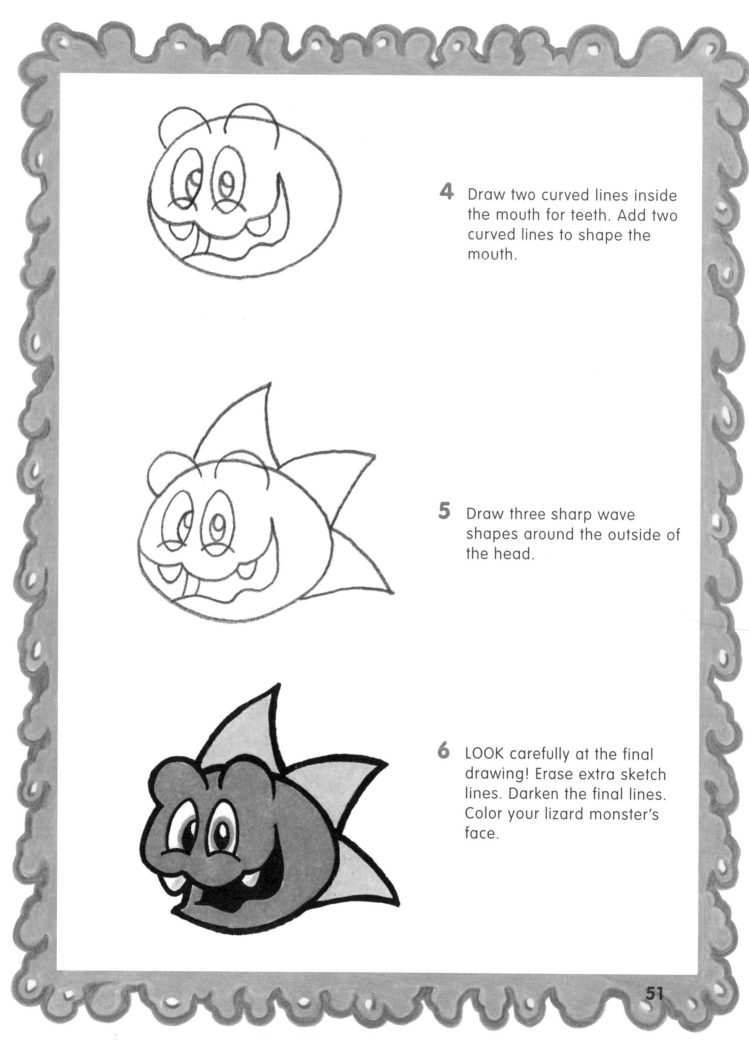

4 Draw two curved lines inside the mouth for teeth. Add two curved lines to shape the mouth.

5 Draw three sharp wave shapes around the outside of the head.

6 LOOK carefully at the final drawing! Erase extra sketch lines. Darken the final lines. Color your lizard monster's face.

51

Let's give the lizard a body!

1 Draw the lizard face again. Add long curved lines for the body. Draw four curved lines for the legs.

2 Add curved lines for arms. Draw ovals for hands. Add curved lines for fingers.

3 Draw small sharp wave shapes for fingernails. Add ovals, at the bottom of the leg lines, for feet.

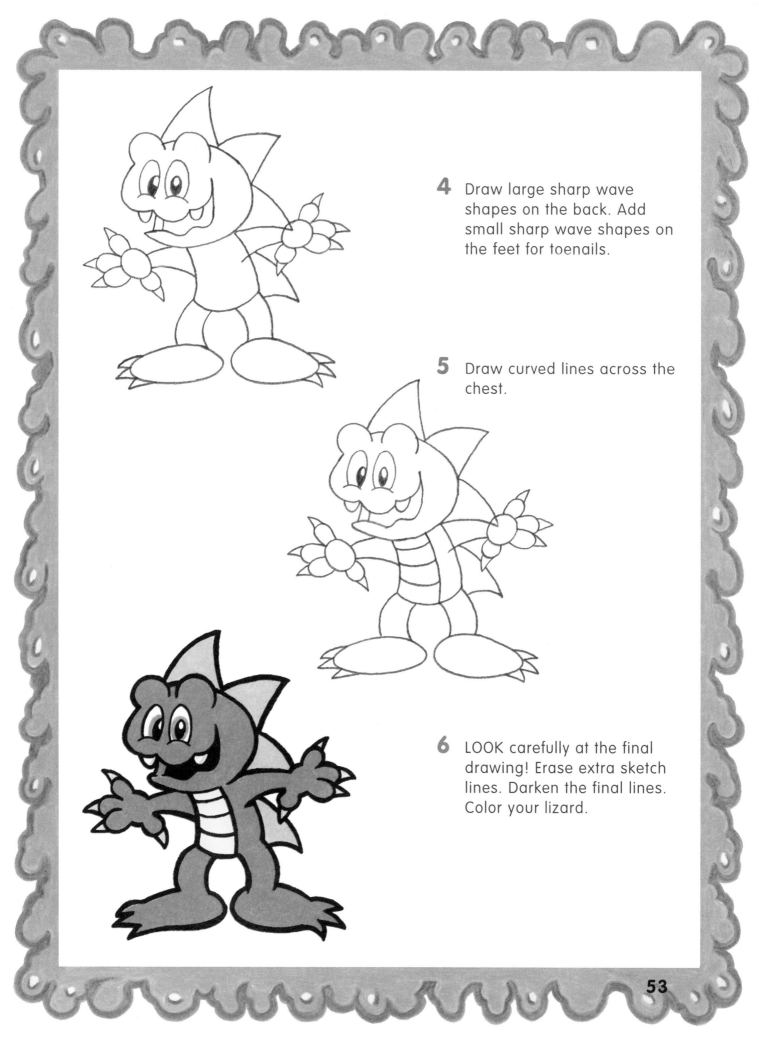

4 Draw large sharp wave shapes on the back. Add small sharp wave shapes on the feet for toenails.

5 Draw curved lines across the chest.

6 LOOK carefully at the final drawing! Erase extra sketch lines. Darken the final lines. Color your lizard.

You can have all kinds of fun drawing monsters. Experiment with different ideas. Let's draw a new lizard monster's face.

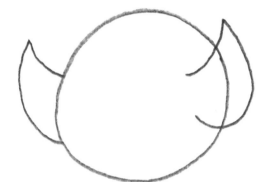

1 Sketch an oval for the head. Draw a sharp wave shape on each side.

2 Sketch curved lines for eyebrows. Draw ovals and curved lines for eyes. Add an oval for a nose.

3 Draw sharp wave shapes for the tops of the eyebrows. Use curved lines to make a mouth.

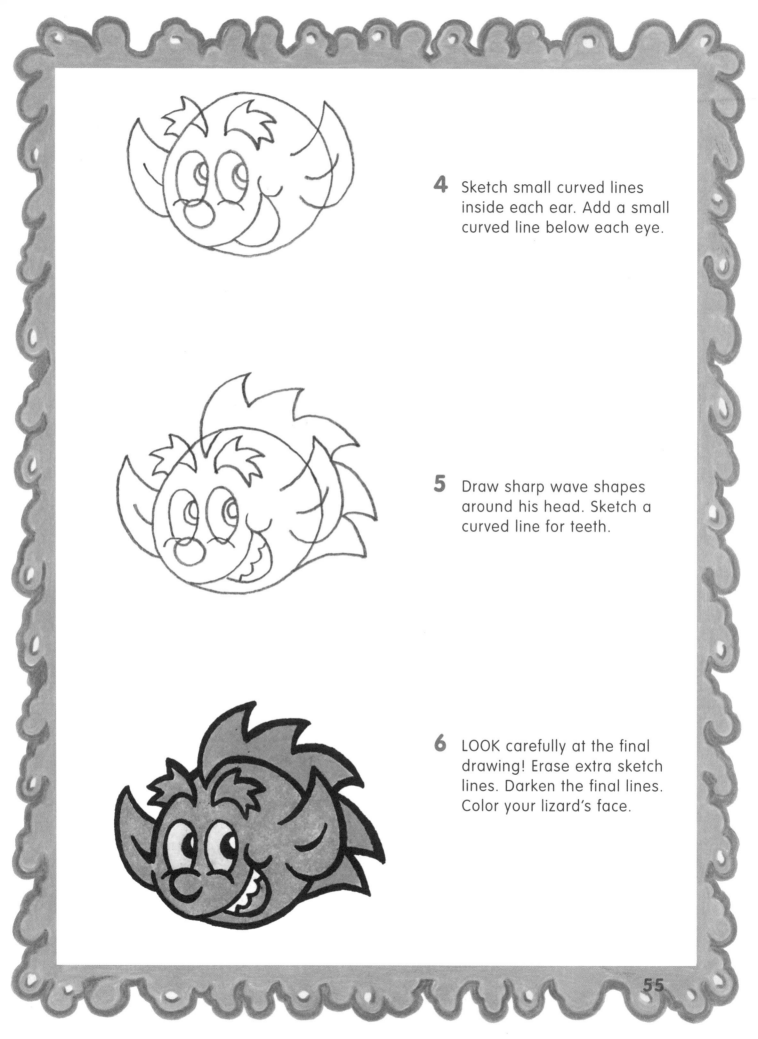

4 Sketch small curved lines inside each ear. Add a small curved line below each eye.

5 Draw sharp wave shapes around his head. Sketch a curved line for teeth.

6 LOOK carefully at the final drawing! Erase extra sketch lines. Darken the final lines. Color your lizard's face.

Monsters can have as many eyes or
hands and feet as you want them to.
Let's draw a different lizard body with
four arms and hands!

1 Draw the monster face, from
page 55, again. Sketch a
long curved line for the body.
Add curved lines for legs.
Draw overlapping ovals for
feet.

2 Sketch a series of straight
lines for the four arms. Add
ovals for hands.

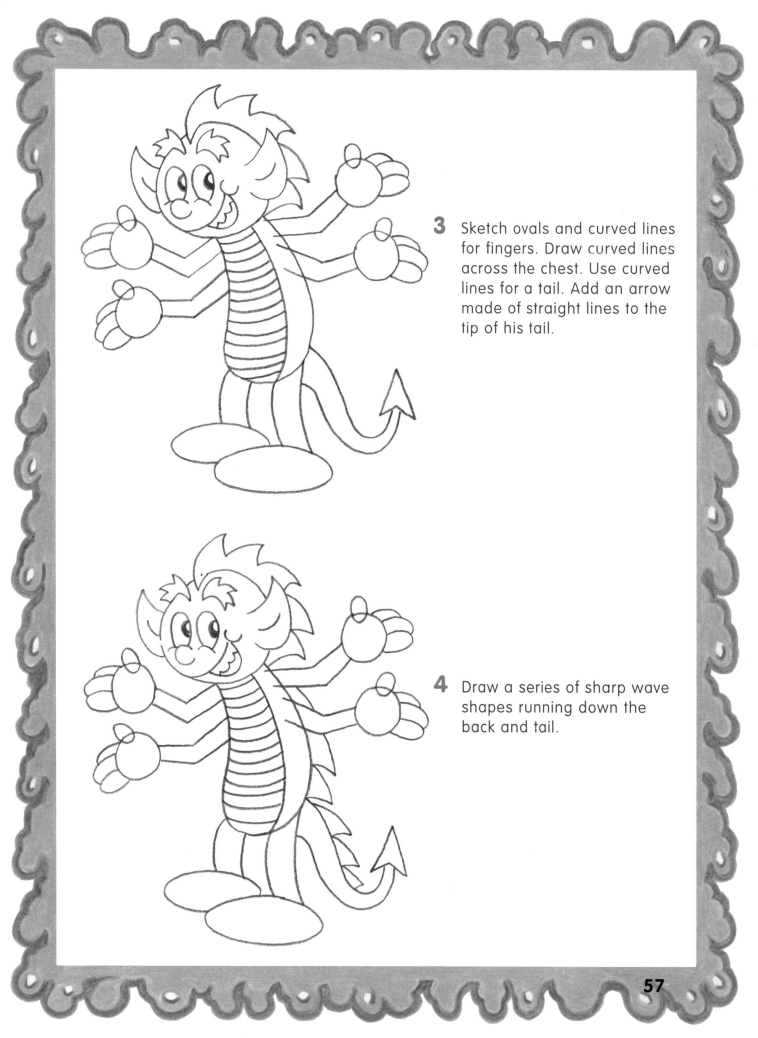

3 Sketch ovals and curved lines for fingers. Draw curved lines across the chest. Use curved lines for a tail. Add an arrow made of straight lines to the tip of his tail.

4 Draw a series of sharp wave shapes running down the back and tail.

5 Add curved lines and ovals for spots on the back and legs. Draw curved lines for toenails.

6 LOOK carefully at the final drawing! Erase extra sketch lines. Darken the final lines. Color your four-armed lizard monster.

If he had a watch on each wrist, he'd have a lot of time on his hands!

More Monsters!!!

Keep going! Look carefully at the basic shapes and lines that give these monsters their unique look. LOOK again, then sketch what you see.

Use the examples on this page to practice, practice, and practice. You will get better and your cartoons will get funnier. Try drawing lots of different monster faces and bodies. Create your own unique cartoon monster

Monster Surprise Game

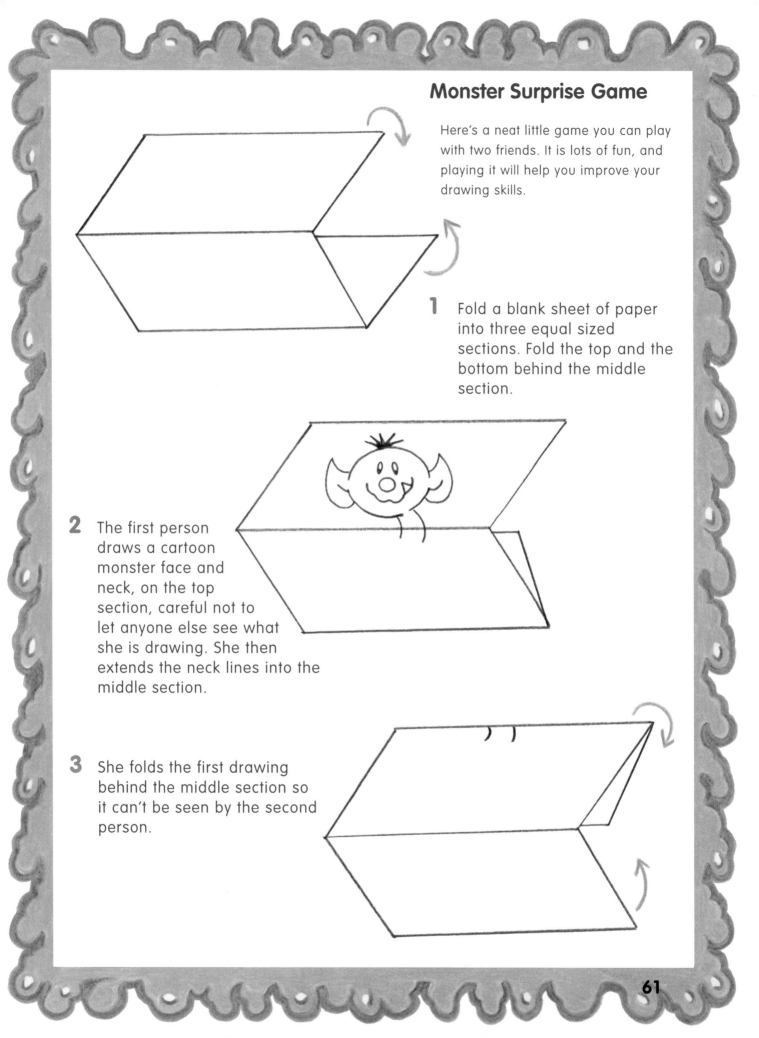

Here's a neat little game you can play with two friends. It is lots of fun, and playing it will help you improve your drawing skills.

1 Fold a blank sheet of paper into three equal sized sections. Fold the top and the bottom behind the middle section.

2 The first person draws a cartoon monster face and neck, on the top section, careful not to let anyone else see what she is drawing. She then extends the neck lines into the middle section.

3 She folds the first drawing behind the middle section so it can't be seen by the second person.

4 The second person draws the body and legs, making sure nobody else sees it, and extends them slightly into the bottom section.

5 The second artist then folds the paper so that just the bottom section shows. The third person draws legs and feet, attaching the legs to the second artist's lines.

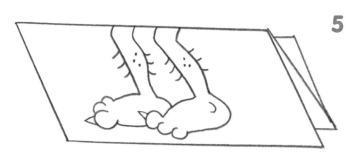

6 Unfold the paper. It's incredible to see the variety of unusual monsters you can create with your friends.

For even more fun, fold three sheets of paper at the same time. Each person gets to draw a head and neck. They then switch sheets with another player, and everyone draws a body. Switch sheets again, and everyone draws legs and feet. This gives everyone something to draw, and you can create three new monsters together at the same time.

Now you're ready to take off on your own! Use what you have learned in this book to create your own wacky cartoon monsters. Draw two or three different monsters and put them together in a scene. Which are happy? Which are sad, or angry, or confused? Can you turn them into a story?

Hmmm....

Award yourself! On the next page you'll find an award certificate you can photocopy to let the world know you're a **Cartoonist's Apprentice First Class!**

Have you enjoyed this book?

Find out about other books in this series and see sample pages online at

www.123draw.com